ENOS PRAYS

To the Golds—Mark, Holly, Kim, Jed, Kyle, and Jessica—with love
Sherrie Johnson

To my wife, LeLe, for her love and patience
Tyler Lybbert

© 1995 Deseret Book Company

All rights reserved. No part of this book may be reproduced in any form or by any means without permission in writing from the publisher, Deseret Book Company, P.O. Box 30178, Salt Lake City, Utah 84130. This work is not an official publication of The Church of Jesus Christ of Latter-day Saints. The views expressed herein are the responsibility of the author and do not necessarily represent the position of the Church or of Deseret Book Company.

Deseret Book is a registered trademark of Deseret Book Company.

Printed in Mexico.

10 9 8 7 6 5 4 3 2 1

ISBN 0-87579-884-5

Designed by Craig Geertsen.

ENOS PRAYS

WRITTEN BY
SHERRIE JOHNSON

ILLUSTRATED BY
TYLER LYBBERT

DESERET BOOK COMPANY
SALT LAKE CITY, UTAH

When Enos was a boy, his father, Jacob, taught him how to pray. He also taught him about faith and the other important things he needed to know about the gospel of Jesus Christ. Enos listened to his father and thought about the things he was taught.

Then one day when Enos was older, he went into the forest to hunt beasts for food. While he was alone, he began to ponder again on the things his father had taught him. He thought about eternal life and the joy of the Saints. The more he thought, the warmer the words of his father burned in his heart and the more he wanted the blessings of the gospel.

Ponder means to think a lot about something.

The desire grew until it was like hunger in his soul. Hunting no longer mattered. He stopped, knelt upon the ground, and cried in mighty prayer that his soul would be saved.

All day long Enos raised his voice in prayer.

Finally Enos received an answer: "Thy sins are forgiven thee, and thou shalt be blessed."

All of the guilt Enos felt was suddenly swept away. In place of the heavy feelings, he now felt the beautiful feelings of love and joy and peace.

Curious, Enos asked the Lord, "How is it done?" The voice answered, "Because of thy faith in Christ, whom thou hast never before heard nor seen. Many years will pass away before Christ shall manifest himself in the flesh. Wherefore, go to. Thy faith hath made thee whole."

But Enos's heart had been changed. He no longer thought only of himself. Now he felt a desire for the welfare of his brethren, the Nephites. He began to pray again, this time for them.

Once more he prayed with all of his might until the voice came into his mind, saying, "I will visit thy brethren according to their diligence in keeping my commandments. If they obey, they will be blessed. If they do not obey, they will bring down sorrow upon their own heads."

When Enos heard these words, his faith grew even stronger. He wanted everyone, even his enemies the Lamanites, to know and feel what he felt and knew. Once more he struggled with all his heart in prayer. This time he asked that a record of the people be preserved.

Enos hoped that in some future day the Lamanites would read the record and know what had happened to their people and to the Nephites. He hoped that this would help them desire to repent and to return to God. He wanted them to have the same happiness and joy that he had found.

After a time the voice again came to Enos:

"I will grant unto thee according to thy desires, because of thy faith."

With these promises Enos returned home.

For the rest of his life, Enos taught the people of Nephi. He prophesied of the things that would come. He testified of the things that he had heard and seen. He tried diligently to restore the Lamanites to the gospel of Jesus Christ, but they would not listen. Instead they sought to destroy the Nephites.

However, Enos knew that he had done all he could do. He had kept the commandments. He had taught the gospel. Therefore he grew old in peace and waited anxiously for the day when he would return to God.

This peace had come to Enos because of his obedience to and faith in Jesus Christ. He knew that when he died he would stand before Jesus Christ. He knew he would look into Jesus' face with pleasure and that he would then hear Jesus say to him, "Come unto me, ye blessed, there is a place prepared for you in the mansions of my Father."